He Walked with Me
and
Talked with Me

He Walked with Me
and
Talked with Me

Bruce Hultgren's Real LIFE
Encounter with Jesus

ANNETTE RODE

XULON PRESS

Xulon Press
2301 Lucien Way #415
Maitland, FL 32751
407.339.4217
www.xulonpress.com

Printed in the United States of America.

Paperback ISBN-13: 978-1-6322-1300-6
eBook ISBN-13: 978-1-6322-1301-3

Dedication

Dedicated to Jesus Christ: Thank you for walking and talking with me, and showing me how REAL You are.

"In the Garden"[1]

Lyrics by C. Austin Miles 1912

I come to the garden alone
While the dew is still on the roses
And the voice I hear, falling on my ear
The Son of God discloses
And He walks with me
And He talks with me
And He tells me I am His own
And the joy we share as we tarry there
None other has ever known

He speaks and the sound of His voice
Is so sweet the birds hush their singing
And the melody that He gave to me
Within my heart is ringing
And He walks with me
And He talks with me
And He tells me I am His own
And the joy we share as we tarry there
None other has ever known

I'd stay in the garden with Him
'Tho the night around me be falling
But He bids me go; through the voice of woe
His voice to me is calling
And He walks with me

And He talks with me
And He tells me I am His own
And the joy we share as we tarry there
None other has ever known

Table of Contents

Acknowledgements

*T*his book is being written fifteen years after my unusual encounter with Jesus Christ. I have shared my story close to home and wherever I have traveled in the United States. Whenever I tell my story in restaurants, bars, churches, on the job, at conferences, etc., I hear comments, "You should write a book" and "You need to put your story in writing." I have always wanted to do that, but since I am not a writer, I didn't know when or if it would happen, until I met Annette.

It has been a pleasure to have a "twin" sister-in-the-Lord, who believes my story and offered to write it. I am incredibly grateful that she believed me and for her willingness to take over the project completely. All I needed to do was recall the details and share. Thank you, Annette, for your dedication and countless hours spent writing this book.

Jim, my co-worker and I spend many hours together and know each other very well. During the encounter with Jesus, he listened to me on a day-to-day basis. I appreciate his heart for God and his honesty. Having a friend to converse with was important during those days of the encounter — and since — when I need to verbalize what is going on in my mind and heart. Jim, you are a true friend and brother-in-the-Lord who understands me. I appreciate having you as an accountability partner.

I am incredibly grateful for the many brothers and sisters in-the-Lord who have given me validation and affirmation upon hearing my unusual story. It is important to be believed in and trusted.

Thank you to my family for your love and support.

I am grateful to Xulon Press for publishing and marketing my story. May God bless you for your dedicated efforts, as you share the love of Jesus throughout the world.

Bruce

———————◆———————

My heart is deeply grateful to You, Holy Spirit, for prompting me to put Bruce's story in writing. It has been a rewarding experience. I have felt Your leading on every step of the journey.

My sincere thanks to you, Bruce – my "twin" — for being fun to work with, and for being patient when I would ask you to repeat parts of the story several times, so I could make sure my notes were accurate. It was important to me that your personality and storytelling manner be preserved and not heavily edited. It was enjoyable to watch you become excited about your unique encounter with Jesus, as if it had happened yesterday.

Heartfelt thanks to Jim, Diane, Sandy, Darin, and John for reading, proofing, editing, offering suggestions, and giving me your needed perspectives.

I pray that this story of Bruce's encounter with Jesus blesses you, the reader. God is impartial and cares about ALL of His children throughout the world. May He reveal Himself to you in a new way as you read and ponder.

Annette

Prologue

One Sunday afternoon in 2007, I (Annette) was shopping for house remodeling supplies at Menards, a large hardware store/lumber yard in Mankato, Minnesota, when I saw Denny, a family friend. During our brief visit, he said he wanted me to meet a brother-in-the-Lord. About that time, Bruce walked over to where we were chatting.

We were introduced and Bruce said, "I saw Jesus Christ."

"Really?" I responded. "Tell me about it."

Right there in the store aisle, Bruce proceeded to tell me a summary of his encounter with Christ. I was intrigued. He was believable and excited about his experience. As I listened, I remember thinking, *I understand why Jesus appeared to you. Your personality is perfect for the message you are sharing.* His persona and manner made him believable.

I didn't see Bruce for quite a while after our initial meeting, until I was pouring punch at my niece's wedding. He came to the punch table and said, "We have something in common."

"What's that?" I replied.

"We have the same birthday. Not just the same date but also the same year, January 15, 1954."

"Really?" I responded. "That's interesting."

I was surprised and thought it was pretty rare to meet someone with the exact same birthdate, who was born approximately a thousand miles away. I was born in Temple, Texas at King's Daughter's Hospital, and Bruce was born in Comfrey, Minnesota at the Comfrey Hospital. Different mothers and fathers, but the same heavenly Father.

In visiting further with Bruce, we found out that we also have similar likes, dislikes, and beliefs.

- We both believe that the Bible, God's Word, is inspired, powerful, and true. It is not just an ancient book of stories; it is spiritual because God is spiritual. It should be read with a spiritual mind-set, or it won't be clearly understood.

  "All Scripture is given by inspiration of God, and is profitable for doctrine, for reproof, for correction,

for instruction in righteousness, that the man of God may be complete, thoroughly equipped for every good work." (2 Timothy 3:16-17, NKJV)

"For the word of God is living and powerful, and sharper than any two-edged sword, piercing even to the division of soul and spirit, and of joints and marrow, and is a discerner of the thoughts and intents of the heart." (Hebrews 4:12, NKJV)

- We both believe that God is the Creator and man was created in His image and likeness.

"In the beginning, God created the heavens and the earth...Then God said, 'Let Us make man in Our image, according to Our likeness; and let them rule over the fish of the sea and over the birds of the sky and over the cattle and over all the earth, and over every creeping thing that creeps on the earth.'" (Genesis 1:1, 26, NASB)

- We both believe in Jesus Christ as our Savior, having been "born again" by God's grace.

"Jesus answered and said to him, 'Most assuredly, I say to you, unless one is born again, he cannot see the kingdom of God.'" (John 3:3, NKJV)

"For by grace you have been saved, through faith, and that not of yourselves, it is the gift of God, not of works lest anyone should boast." (Ephesians 2:8-9, NKJV)

- We both believe in the power of the Holy Spirit to transform and sanctify our hearts and lives to become more like Christ.

"But the fruit of the Spirit is love, joy, peace, patience, kindness, goodness, faithfulness, gentleness, self-control. Against such there is no law." (Galatians 5:22-23, ESV)

- We both believe that love is the fulfillment of the Law.

"For the entire law is fulfilled in keeping this one command: "Love your neighbor as yourself." If you bite and devour each other, watch out or you will be destroyed by each other. So, I say, walk by the Spirit, and you will not gratify the desires of the flesh." (Galatians 5:14-16, NIV)

- We both believe in the sovereignty of God. There are no coincidences but rather divine appointments, opportunities, and connections. Things don't "just happen" ... we are not "lucky" but, rather, we are blessed by God.

"For from Him and through Him and to Him
are all things. To Him be glory forever. Amen."
(Romans 11:36, ESV)

Bruce's very unusual experience was life-changing. He has been obedient to the heavenly Father by sharing his story wherever he goes, as the Spirit directs him. Many people have asked him to put his story in writing. That is not his forte; however, by his own admission, Bruce is a storyteller.

It is no coincidence that I love reading books and have always wanted to write a book. When I heard Bruce's story, and then found out that we were "twins," I knew that this was a story that needed to be written; and it was a story I would enjoy writing.

I was curious about my "twin" and about this man Jesus chose to appear to in our modern world, so I began to ask him questions about his life.

This book is Bruce's true, real-life, personal experience, as he told it to me.

Annette Rode

The Early Years

"But you must continue in the things which you have learned and been assured of, knowing from whom you have learned them, and that from childhood you have known the Holy Scriptures, which are able to make you wise for salvation through faith which is in Christ Jesus." (2 Timothy 3:14-15, NKJV)

My Hultgren ancestors came from Sweden; my grandfather married a full-blooded German. I have four brothers and one sister, being the second to the oldest child. Farm chores included feeding the chickens, gathering eggs, mowing grass, feeding cattle and hogs, etc. I went to St. James School, from grades 1-12, and was involved in football, wrestling, and baseball.

My parents were highly involved in Lutheran Church activities, serving on church boards and Ladies Aid. We attended church services regularly as a family. I started Sunday school at age four and attended through my freshman year in high school, then I was confirmed. In my junior year, I taught third-grade Sunday school.

West Svedahl Lutheran Church

The summer after my high school graduation, my brother and I were hired by my cousin to help put up grain bins in the Windom, Minnesota area. That fall, I helped Dad harvest crops, since I was still living at home with my parents. It was right after harvest and I was reading my Bible. I went to bed and was sleeping, then I was awakened and could see my grandfather walk into the bedroom. I sat there watching and got scared. I thought, *I need to get up, turn on the light and see if this is real.* I couldn't move, couldn't lift my body. A few seconds later, I was able to move. I got up and turned the light on, but he wasn't there. I told my mother about the experience because it was so real. However, my grandpa was still alive, so my mother didn't know what it was.

I continued to find various carpentry jobs, helping relatives in different locations. The drinking age was nineteen, so I was able to go into bars and drink with my cousin when we played pool. While we were working in St. Cloud, Minnesota, we went to parties to meet people and had fun drinking, dancing, and meeting women, including twin sisters Diane and Darlene.

When my grandfather Hultgren died five days before my twenty-first birthday, I was living and working at my parents' home because they wanted me to do some siding, build cabinets, and remodel the bathroom. My grandfather was like a father to me. We were very close, having worked together on the farm. He was there all the time and had a lot of patience with us, unlike my father. On my twenty-first birthday, I had a revelation that I needed to become a man, settle down, strap up my boots, and man up.

After the funeral and finishing some work we were doing on the farmhouse, I went back to St. Cloud. My cousin and I went to the bar and saw Diane and Darlene. I was interested in a relationship with Diane. While we were all out as a group, my cousin became interested in Darlene. My cousin and I ended up dating the twin girls and both couples got married at the same place, same time, same wedding. I was age twenty-two.

My wife Diane and I lived in a house we bought in Sveadahl, Minnesota that was located about a block from our church. We were blessed with two girls. Life was based around the church, my family, and construction work.

I started my own carpentry business at the age of thirty, the same age Jesus was when He began His ministry. I had made the decision at age nineteen to become a carpenter, because Jesus was a carpenter. I had dreams of preaching the Gospel in the wilderness. Sometimes when I was working in my woodshop, I would see a light but didn't understand it. Often, I would sing church hymns as I worked. I knew the Father was speaking to me at different times, but I didn't feel compelled to tell anyone.

Bruce in his work truck

When I was thirty-five, I was interested in buying the family farm that was for sale. I prayed for guidance. I actually went to the farm, and knelt down and asked God how I could do this. My wife and I were church custodians for a few years. One Sunday we were preparing the altar, turning on the sound booth, putting up hymn numbers, and lighting candles for the service. I heard the Lord speak to me; He told me what to do so I could buy the farm. I did what He told me to do and it all worked out well. We moved to the home farm in 1990 and are still living there today. In 2013, our family built a new house on our fifth-generation family farm that has been in the Hultgren family since 1883.

I have always prayed that God would guide and strengthen me to face the challenges I had in business. When I worked for elderly people, I would sit down and visit with them, providing them fellowship and doing extra chores for them. Sometimes I would take them out to eat to get them out of the house and spend time with them. The elderly needed someone to care for them. God put it in my heart and mind to be that person – to lend them a helping hand.

Now and then, during my thirties and forties, I had night dreams of proclaiming the second coming of Christ. I never told anyone because I thought they were "just dreams."

In the fall of 2004, my co-worker Jim and I went to a Christian meeting about the Muslim religion where a former Muslim was speaking; he was talking about his birth religion. When asked how he became a Christian, he responded, "I was in a school and opened a door, and saw a group of people studying the Bible. They invited me to study with them. I found out the Koran was similar to the Old Testament. I kept going to classes and found them interesting."

Jim said one time he had a great shaking come on him. He had a vision and Jesus Christ appeared to him, held out His hand, and said, "Come unto Me." So, he did. He became a Christian right then and there. I knew he was telling the truth and felt a strong connection in my spirit with him.

Quite often through the years of my life, when I was worshipping and singing in a church service, I felt the power of the Holy Spirit come on me. It was extremely strong and powerful, like energy in my hands.

Now I will tell you about my most unusual, yet real, experience.

He Walked and Talked with Me

*"And they said to one another, Did not our hearts
burn within us, while He talked with us by the
way, and while he opened to us the scriptures?"
(Luke 24:32, KJV)*

Day One – Tuesday, May 10, 2005

At a place south of Butterfield, Minnesota, where Jim and I were working, I had great fear come on me. I told Jim I had great fear and couldn't figure out why or where it was coming from.

At noon, we were outside in the yard and Jim said, "There's a spiritual battle going on over you."

Then I prayed and meditated. I went back to work and was praying, and just like that, I heard this word in my spirit: "I am the Messiah."

He kept saying that to me. I was debating if I was hearing it in my own power and if my own mind was saying it.

Then I heard, "I am the Messiah. I am the God of Abraham, Isaac, and Jacob." This is when I knew the Almighty was speaking to me.

> *"that they may believe that the Lord God of their fathers, the God of Abraham, the God of Isaac, and the God of Jacob, has appeared to you."* (Exodus 4:5, NKJV)

> *'I am the God of Abraham, the God of Isaac, and the God of Jacob'? God is not the God of the dead, but of the living."* (Matthew 22:32, NKJV)

My head went backwards and, to my right, I saw a white light. I turned my head toward the light and that's when I saw Jesus Christ standing before me. It was a full image of a man. I could see His light brown sandals and His light brown hair, down to his shoulders in length. He was wearing a pure white, wool robe that came down to just below His knees. There was a three-inch white border on all of the edges of the robe, including around the sleeves. His hair wasn't combed smooth. I could see shimmers of red in his hair, but I couldn't see His face. I could see the outline of His face, but his face lacked detail – it was fuzzy and unclear, like white particles. I kept turning to look, as I was working and He was standing there watching me. I was curious and amazed because this was an unusual experience. I was thinking, *Is this real?*

When I turned to the west, I saw Him. Then I turned south *(checking to see if my eyes were playing tricks on me),* then I turned east and then north. It is only when I looked west that I saw Him. I said, "There You are."

I went over to Jim because I had to cut a board and I told him, "I have quite an experience going on."

Jim said, "What's that?"

"The Messiah is here."

"He is? What does He want?"

"Well, I don't have to ask Him what He wants. He's here to watch over me. Can't you see Him?"

"No, He's in you. He's revealing Himself to you."

"Oh," I said.

As I was working and as I turned toward Him, I felt I was being cleansed. I used my hands and received the cleansing, as if I was washing my face with water. It's His blood that cleanses us from our sin. I didn't see blood, but I knew in my spirit I was cleansed by the blood of the Lamb.

> *"For you know that it was not with perishable things such as silver or gold that you were redeemed from the empty way of life handed down to you from your ancestors, but with the precious blood of Christ, a lamb without blemish or defect." (1 Peter 1:18-19, NIV)*

After I was cleansed, Jesus said to me, "Why can't you see My face?" *(He was arousing my curiosity and wanting me to draw closer to Him.)*

I said, "Why can't I?" I was searching into His face, concentrating, looking deeply, trying to see more facial details. Then when I met Him eye to eye, I felt the fire of God's Spirit go into my being through my eyes, permeating my brain, flowing to the back of my head. My eyes burned for three days. I could feel His Spirit go into my soul. It was divine energy that powerfully embraced my being; it was a "baptism of fire."

> *"As for me (John the Baptist), I baptize you with water for repentance, but He who is coming after me is mightier than I, and I am not fit to remove His sandals; He will baptize you with the Holy Spirit and fire." (Matthew 3:11, NASB)*

After that experience, my eyes were burning. I went to Jim and said, "My eyes are burning."

He had me look into his face and said, "This is way out of my league. You need to talk to Stephen Jones. I've never heard of anything like that." Neither of us knew what was going on. *(Dr. Stephen Jones is a historian, Bible teacher, and author that we both know and respect.)*

On our way home that evening, Jim wanted to stop at a friend's house. We stopped over at Howard's house and were visiting out on his deck. When Howard went inside to get something, Jim asked, "Can you see Him?"

"Yes, I can see Him," I told Jim. "He's sitting on your lap."

"He is?"

"Yes," I said, "I can see Him sitting on your lap."

"I can't sense Him," Jim replied.

It was time to go home, but before leaving, Jim said, "We'll see what you see tomorrow. You'd better not tell anybody because they'll think you're crazy."

That night, I didn't say anything to my wife and sister-in-law.

Day Two – Wednesday, May 11, 2005

The next morning, I went to look in the mirror and noticed a white spot in my right eye. Then I went into the kitchen and was so excited that I had seen the Messiah that I grabbed my wife and hugged and kissed her, and I hugged my sister-in-law. After the hugs, I told them, "I saw Jesus Christ."

Their response was, "What has gotten into you?" They were puzzled about my excitement. We didn't talk about it anymore that morning.

I went outside to get my chainsaw to cut up some trees on the farm. I could see Jesus as I walked in the sunlight. He was walking on my right side, plain as day, in living color. I thought, *How real is this?*

He walked with me wherever I went. I looked down as we were walking to the north, on the east side of the machine shed. I saw His robe move right with the north wind. When I picked up my chainsaw to begin cutting trees, I told Jesus to stand back away from the chainsaw because I didn't want to hurt Him. He looked so real in living color, as He stood there watching me cut a tree. Then I set the chainsaw down and I was going to pull on a branch. The next thing I knew, His robe was right in front of me. All I could see was His white robe. I realized that He was pulling the branch with me. We got done with that and I walked over to the water hydrant to wash off my rubber overshoes, because it was muddy out there in the field. As I walked, I could see Him walking to my right side. I washed off my rubber overshoes and came back, and He was still walking right with me.

Then I looked down, and His Spirit morphed into me and then came out. When He came out, He was carrying me; He had my spiritual body in His arms. He was carrying me like "footprints in the sand." I was still walking in the flesh as I saw this. The next thing I knew He morphed back into me and went out again, and He was walking by Himself. After that experience, I thought, *Who am I to have this happening to me?* I sat in the pickup to wait for Jim.

Jim got in the pickup and said, "Can you see Him?"

"Yes, He's sitting between us. He's going to work with us."

"Oh," Jim said.

When we went to work, I could see Him. He was standing 10-15 feet away, just watching us as we worked and He'd say something funny. He has a very good sense of humor. I started laughing and Jim would say, "What's so funny?"

I said, "Well, He said something funny to me."

Jim commented, "Well, I've read books where Jesus was humorous."

I could see all these things. He was continually trying to make me relaxed and comfortable in His presence, like being with the best friend you have had in your life.

Day Three – Thursday, May 12, 2005

I was thinking about the fact that I needed to tell my pastor I saw Jesus. I was heading outside before work on Thursday, May 12 when I heard from Jesus in the Spirit, "Wash her feet."

I thought, *Oh boy. I've never done that before. I'd better pray about this.*

So, I prayed about it in my shop. The next thing I knew, I saw a vision of myself washing my pastor's feet. Jesus was standing on my right side, watching me wash her feet. When Jim came into the shop, I told him what I had heard and seen in the vision.

Jim said, "Jesus wants you to wash her feet."

"Oh boy," I said. Then we headed to work.

That afternoon my pastor called me to talk about the Sunday service, since I was chair of the congregation. I told her, "I have something very interesting to tell you."

She said, "What is it? You've been making some unusual statements lately." *(Statements like "if this cup could pass, let it" because of challenges in the church.)*

15

"I can't tell you over the phone," I replied. I set up an appointment to meet with her on Friday evening. When I hung up the phone, I thought, *Oh boy,* knowing I was going to tell her about seeing Jesus.

I was also able to see in the spirit that there was a spiritual battle going on between my pastor and I. I saw in the spirit that we were discussing about me seeing Jesus Christ.

When Jim heard that I had seen my discussion with the pastor in the spirit, he said, "That's a spiritual battle going on. You need to go into that spiritual battle."

When I went into the battle, I saw Jesus stand to my right. He morphed into me and then I stepped back, and my pastor was actually talking with Jesus Christ, while thinking she was talking to me because she couldn't see Him like I could. I laughed because I knew she thought she was talking to me, but she was talking to Christ.

"What's so funny?" Jim asked.

"She's talking with Jesus, but she thinks she's talking with me."

After that, I heard, "Hallelujah, Hallelujah!!" I told Jim.

"The battle's been won," he said.

That same evening, we had a church council meeting. I was sitting on one end of the table as chairman; the other members were sitting at the other end of the table. The pastor sat with them and had devotions and prayer to begin the meeting. When she started devotions, in my spirit, I could feel buckets of water being poured on me. Water is the symbol of the Holy Spirit. I knew that was confirmation the battle was done. I knew when I spoke with her on Friday evening about seeing Jesus that she would believe me. The battle was won!

Day Four – Friday, May 13, 2005

When I got up to dress, Jesus was sitting next to me on the left side of the bed. He asked what I was going to do that day because it was raining. I replied that I was going to work in the shop and asked if that was OK. He didn't reply. I could see Jesus with me in the shop, watching me work. It was a normal day; nothing real unusual, other than seeing Jesus there with me.

That evening, I went to the West Sveadahl church to keep the appointment I made with my pastor. I was carrying a plastic container, a quart bottle of lukewarm water, and a towel when I met her in the narthex (lobby) of the church. Jim told me to wear white so I wore white clothing. When I walked in, she said, "What do you have there?"

"Oh, you'll see," I replied.

We went into her office and she sat down in her chair. I swung her chair around to face me, as I was kneeling on the floor. I told her I was in prayer and Jesus told me to wash her feet.

"I'm not denying Jesus Christ," she said. She took off her shoes and socks, and put her feet in the basin. I washed her feet one at a time.

I had my head down in my kneeling position as I was drying her feet. Then, after I was done, I looked at her and said, "I've seen Jesus Christ."

Her eyes got as big as saucers. I told her about Jesus morphing into me with a baptism of fire and she exclaimed, "He came into you!"

She had me stand up and go sit in a chair, and then I told her my story of the past two days. She said, "I believe you, Bruce."

Then she said, "Let's go into prayer." After the prayer, I went home.

Day Five – Saturday, May 14, 2005

I went to a children's dance recital of a four-year-old neighbor. She invited me because we had done work for her parents and we got along very well. Jim came along so we could go immediately to work after the recital. We went into the auditorium and sat down. I wasn't expecting anything. Just like that, I could feel the Holy Spirit come upon me – just an overwhelming love of the children who were there. I could see the Spirit of Jesus go and hug the children. My heart was just melting. I had tears in my eyes, as this was going on.

I asked Jim, "Can you feel this?"

He said, "No," so he went into meditation and prayer. As I saw him in prayer, I prayed for the will of the Father so Jim could experience this.

Just like that, Jim turned to me and said, "Boy, this is divine power!"

I said, "I know." It was so powerful I could feel the Spirit just like a mist of rain coming down from heaven and covering the whole building. The Spirit was incredibly strong during the entire program.

Day Six – Sunday, May 15, 2005

I was supposed to light the candles on the altar at church before the morning service. The pastor was in her waiting room on the side of the altar, preparing for the service. When I went in to get the lighter, I mentioned to the pastor to please not tell anyone yet what I had shared with her about seeing Jesus. She agreed.

The pastor came down the aisle as the congregation was singing the last verse of the closing hymn, "Here I am Lord. Is it I, Lord?" [2]

I was standing in the back pew and could see the tears in her eyes. It seemed to me that because she knew I was called by the heavenly Father to be His messenger, the words of the song impacted her.

Later that morning, she commented, "I hope your wife is ready for the calling God has for you."

Day Seven – Monday, May 16, 2005

The next day as I was working, I noticed a group of particles off to my right. It looked like a small person. I searched into that substance of particles to see who it was and realized it was my niece, Natalie. I said, "Oh my goodness, that's Natalie!" She passed away about two and a half years previous to this. *(When the Father speaks to me, He speaks by His Spirit to my spirit. The more I hear His voice, the easier it is to recognize.)*

I tried to communicate with Natalie. When I didn't hear anything, I ignored it and walked around the sawhorses we used on the job. I saw her substance had moved off to the side, so I started back to work putting on siding. I walked along the sawhorses to go to my trailer, which was off to my left; there was the substance walking again. I knew it was

Natalie. As I was walking, I saw my left foot go ahead. In other words, my spirit walked before me. I went and picked "Natalie" up and carried her, hugged and kissed her. When I set her down, my spiritual being came back into me. Since I was also still walking in the flesh, I saw my spirit doing all of this. Then I went back to the trailer and told Jim everything that had happened.

"I've never heard of anything like that," he said.

I went home and told my wife Diane, "I saw Natalie." I also said, "I wonder if I'll see Daniel."

Day Eight – Tuesday, May 17, 2005

The following day, I noticed something on my right side again – a distance from me. I thought, *Well, who's that? There's somebody out there.* I looked – searching deeply into the substance and pretty soon the next thing I knew it was Daniel, my wife's brother who died two years earlier. I tried to communicate with him, but he didn't communicate with me. Then I walked on the porch where I was going to put some siding on. I went off to the right and knelt down. I noticed the substance followed me and the next thing I knew, the substance was to my left.

It said to me, "Tell my wife, Barb, I love her and give her a hug and kiss for me, and tell the rest of the family that I'm OK."

Then I turned and said, "Ok, Daniel." He disappeared just like that.

Those were my experiences during the eight days in May of 2005 when Jesus became very real to me. He answered my prayer and released me of the fear that was overwhelming me.

Go and Tell

> *"For I am not ashamed of the gospel of Christ, for it is the power of God to salvation for everyone who believes, to the Jew first, and also to the Greek." (Romans 1:16, NKJV)*

There were more experiences after the initial eight-day encounters. With each encounter, vision, dream, and hearing God's Spirit speak to me in many and varied ways, He became, and still becomes, more real every day. I am firmly convinced that God loves me; that He loves all mankind unconditionally and that we don't need to fear. He is with us every moment and cares about us. He wants to have a loving relationship with each of us.

Who in My Family Can I Tell?

At first, I wasn't going to say anything to anyone because I figured they would think I was crazy.

On Sunday, May 22, 2005, we went to church. After communion, we sang: "Thank the Lord and sing His praise; tell everyone what He has done."

While I was singing the song, I KNEW in my heart that Jesus wanted me to tell people the experience I had with Him.

After the service, I got in the car to go to a graduation party in the Twin Cities. The song kept repeating in my mind; I was being prompted by the Holy Spirit to share.

I thought, *I can't tell my dad now. Who in my family can I tell?* I thought of my brother-in-law and realized that I should tell him first. We were traveling to his son's graduation party, so I knew I'd see him soon.

When we arrived, I told my brother-in-law that I needed to talk to him privately. After the graduation party ended and the guests left, he and I went into his bedroom and I shared my story. His eyes got as big as saucers. When I told him, I saw Jesus Christ, he said, "I believe you, Bruce."

Besides my wife, sister-in-law, and Jim, this was the first time the circle got bigger. I knew it was time to share with others.

My parents were in the living room and were wondering, out of curiosity, what I had told my brother-in-law. I shared my story with them and my dad broke down in tears. Both of my parents believed me. I hugged and kissed my dad, mom, and sister.

"What brought this on?" my mom asked.

I told her I had prayed to be released from fear and God answered my prayer in a very unusual way. After this point in time, the opportunities to share continued and it became easier to talk about. I knew that not everyone would accept or believe my story, but I shouldn't get discouraged. I needed to keep sharing and remain humble, knowing this was a gift from God.

Dancing on the Altar

On June 12, 2005, I went to tell my children in Rochester, Minnesota. We went to church and as the organ started playing, it took me into a higher spiritual level. I could see Jesus, the Messiah, in the front of the church, dancing on the altar. I said to my daughter, "I can see Jesus."

"Where?" she asked.

"He's dancing on the altar," I replied. I could feel the Holy Spirit come onto me, very, very powerfully.

Then afterwards, we went to the grocery store and I could sense the Messiah was walking with us. I even told my daughters, "He's walking with us."

Groomed for the Wedding

I went to my niece's wedding on July 16, 2005. As the organ started playing, I could feel the Holy Spirit come upon me; I could feel His blessing. Just like that, I could see the Messiah ten feet up in the air standing there, all groomed for the wedding. He was floating up in the air wearing a linen robe. It was white with no borders, came just below His knees and had long sleeves all the way to His wrists. Through it all, I could feel the Holy Spirit very strong and powerful.

Visiting Daniel's Grave

On August 14, 2005, I was in St. Cloud with some relatives. We went out to see my brother-in-law Daniel's gravestone for the first time. My sister-in-law was taking pictures. I wasn't expecting anything; I was reading the inscription on the gravestone. On the bottom of the stone was inscribed, "In the loving arms of Jesus." When I read those words, I was immediately surrounded by the Spirit, like a veil enveloping me. The divine power came upon me and I saw the Messiah standing next to Danny's stone for about ten minutes. I could feel the power of the Spirit with me very strongly that day as I walked in the cemetery. It was like I was in another world in my spirit, but at the same time, in my body, I could still hear conversations going on between those who were there with me.

Go Forward and Tell

There are still many times when I can feel the Spirit. He told me that I was to go forward and tell people – like the Post Communion Canticle lyrics in the green Lutheran Book of Worship say: "Thank the Lord and sing His praise, tell everyone what He has done." ³

Why Can't I Talk to God and Work?

In the fall of 2005, at a neighbor's farm, I was laying block on the foundation for his garage. Harold, his dad, was handing me the block. I heard in the spirit, "Word of life, Jesus Christ."

I told Harold, "God is talking with me."

"How can you talk to God and work?"

"I talk to you and work, why can't I talk to God and work?" Then I thought, *Where is this coming from? I should know where this is coming from.* Then the thought came to me, *It's coming from the blue book – With One Voice.*

As soon as work ended at five pm, I took Jim to my place to get his truck and then drove to the church to get the blue book. I knew the answer was there to interpret what Christ was trying to tell me. It was the Gospel Acclamation on page 48: "Word of life, Jesus Christ, all glory to you!" ⁴

That was the message I was given. Jesus keeps showing me His approval, as I go out to tell people about Him, His character, and what it's like to be with Him.

I took the blue book and showed Jim to prove to him that God is really talking to me, using the Scriptures in the worship hymnal.

He said, "He's talking with you. That's pretty powerful. You'd better not say too much about that because that's a powerful statement."

"I know God's talking to me," I replied.

Dramatic Life Change

"For the Lord GOD helps Me, Therefore, I am not disgraced; Therefore, I have set My face like flint, And I know that I will not be ashamed." (Isaiah 50:7, NASB)

God was teaching me to be very aware of His presence and listen for His voice speaking to me.

Keep the Sabbath Day Holy

I came home from a church service one Sunday and decided to go out and mow the lawn. I was mowing and singing the last song we sang in the service when, about ten feet away, I saw Jesus looking at me. Every way I turned, I could see His eyes watching me for about five or ten minutes. That night when I went to bed, I heard Him speak to me three times, saying, "Keep the Sabbath day holy."

The Right Direction

In 2005, about a month after Jesus told me to go out and tell people about seeing Him, I asked for confirmation if I was doing this right. The next day, I could hear music playing a familiar tune in my head; just one line of music. At first, I couldn't identify what the song was. Later that day, I sat down to watch *America's Got Talent* with my wife and the people started singing "Daydream Believer" – the song I heard in my head earlier that day. The family was named the Wright family. God confirmed that I was headed in the **right** direction.

Spread the Gospel

Another message came to me through song lyrics from the Lutheran Book of Worship written by George W. Kitchin: "Lift High the Cross, the love of Christ Proclaim." [5]

He was telling me to go forward to spread the gospel and the personal experiences that I had with Jesus Christ. I prayed to the Father, asking if this was His will. He gave me two messages: "Go, My children with My blessing, I will be there with you," and the other message, "Unite them in prayer and give them a foretaste of the feast to come," reminding me of the offertory communion praise I learned. I went before the St. James ministerial and told my story. I leave it up to the Father and go when He gives me the command to go forward. I do not step out before Him on my own.

Keys Found

I was visiting my daughter, Jessica, and helping build an addition on their house. After lunch, I laid down on the couch for a short nap. When I got up, I went to get something out of the truck, but it was locked and the keys weren't in my pocket. I worked on the skid loader for a while and said, "Father, I need You to help me find those keys." Pretty soon, I heard, "Under the couch." I thought, *Under the couch?* I jumped off the skid loader, ran into the house, and took the cushions off the couch, but the keys weren't there. Then I remembered He said, "**Under** the couch." I picked up the couch and, sure enough, there were the keys. I was on my knees, so I thanked the Heavenly Father for telling me where they were.

"Why Don't You Pray?"

I was at home and was going to put gas in the tractor so I could mow the CRP *(Conservation Reserve Program)* field. I was mowing the whole 2.5 acres out by the driveway, then mowed a different field that was not as smooth, so the tractor was bouncing around. Just like that I noticed that the gas was splashing off the top of the tractor. I stopped and muttered to myself, "Where's the cap?" I pulled up to the house and decided to go in and have some coffee.

I told my wife Diane, "I lost the gas cap."

"I'll come out and help you look for it," she said.

I walked into the field and looked; Diane walked in another area. I went to the other field and we walked around but didn't find it. Then we both came back and I said, "There's supposed to be another cap in the shed."

She said, "Why don't you pray about it? Maybe the Father will tell you where it is."

I chuckled and skeptically thought, *I don't know. OK.* I meditated and silently asked the Father, *Can you help me out so I can find out where the gas cap is?* What I heard was, *"Walk backward."* I thought, *Walk backward? Am I hearing things? Wait a minute. Really? Well, OK.* I thought about that, and I was really in doubt because I wondered how you can walk backward in the field. So, I made a big circle around the field and went backward to where I came into the field. As soon as I was walking closer to where I had entered the field, I saw a flashing, shining light; it caught my eye. I kept walking toward the light and, sure enough, that was the gas cap. The reason why the Father had me go backward into the field was because of how it was lying on the ground. The sun shining to the east caught the metal inside of the cap just right, due to the reflection from the sun. Walking the other direction, I would have walked right over it and would not have seen it. Because I walked backward, I caught the glimmer with my eyes. When I found the cap, I dropped to my knees right there and thanked the

Father. I picked it up and hollered at Diane, who was in the shed still searching, "I found it."

"You did?" she exclaimed.

"Yes, you told me to pray and the heavenly Father showed me where to go, and here it is."

The Tree of Life and The Courtroom

In 2008, I was at a spiritual conference in Arkansas. Early Sunday morning, I went into the spirit and was looking inside me, and saw a door open. The light drew me. I saw white clouds. As I went deeper beyond the door, I came to a clearing and saw the Tree of Life. The leaves were full, brilliant green in color; it was very beautiful. This area closed and then I was taken to another area where I saw a big chair, like a courtroom chair. There was a brilliant, glowing light at the back of the chair. Then I saw the light grow brighter and brighter. It kept coming toward me through the back of the chair. I realized the face coming toward me was my own face. Then, I saw myself sitting in the chair with my arms on the armrest. I could not see anything to my right, but as far as I could see to my left were elderly, white-haired men sitting in similar chairs, all looking straight ahead with their arms on the chair armrests just like me. They were dressed in modern attire. When I reflected on this vision, it reminded me of an earlier vision where I saw flashcards with pictures of men from the past, because of the attire they were wearing. The flashcards were in front of me and on my right. The flash-card vision was about overcomers sitting in judgement over the world. The elderly, white-haired men sitting in chairs on my left were also modern-day overcomers.

When I went back to the conference, I told Jim what I saw. He said, "You saw the Tree of Life and you were sitting in a judgement chair."

The Tree of Life represents the cleansing of the nations; that's what the conference was all about.

> *"And he who overcomes, and keeps My works until the end, to him I will give power over the nations." (Revelation 2:26, NKJV)*

> *"To him who overcomes I will grant to sit with Me on My throne, as I also overcame and sat down with My Father on His throne." (Revelation 3:21, NKJV)*

> *"Do you not know that the saints will judge the world? And if the world will be judged by you, are you unworthy to judge the smallest matters? Do you not know that we shall judge angels? How much more, things that pertain to this life?" (1 Corinthians 6:2-3, NKJV)*

"And the things that you have heard from me among many witnesses, commit these to faithful men who will be able to teach others also." (2 Timothy 2:2, NKJV)

Evil Spirits Removed

One night, I got down on my hands and knees and asked the Father to remove all evil spirits within me. When I went to bed, I dreamt I was walking with another person along a ditch. The other person was walking by the edge of the field, and I was walking down in the ditch with a garden rake in my hand. As we walked along, the other person to my right said, "There's a snake in that hole." When I came to the hole in question, a large snake with an alligator head came out. It went straight up in the air about ten feet, then flopped to the ground on my right side. I took my garden rake and killed it. My interpretation is that God's Spirit in me killed the evil spirits as I had asked Him.

Building the House of God

I was at a conference in the Twin Cities, staying with my sister. In the early morning, I was moving in and out of sleep before I got up. I saw a house that was partially built. Part of the house had rafters. The framework was up. I could see into the house and noticed a man kneeling down, pounding nails in the floor. The interpretation is that I'm the carpenter; the Kingdom of God is the house being built.

I am one of His messengers to spread the Word of God and build the house of God.

> *"For the Kingdom of God is not just a lot of talk; it is living by God's power." (1 Corinthians 4:20, NLT)*

> *"For the kingdom of God is not a matter of eating and drinking, but of righteousness, peace, and joy in the Holy Spirit." (Romans 14:17, BSB)*

Being Fed by the Father

I was down on my knees praying to the Father, always wanting to be fed <u>by Him</u> – making sure I was not misled or deceived. During the night, I woke up and saw dark clouds in my bedroom. Out of the big, black cloud came a huge raven. I put my hands up to see and realized it was all spiritual and felt eerie. The raven fed Elijah. This was a symbol/sign from the heavenly Father that <u>He was</u> feeding me.

> *"The ravens brought him (Elijah) bread and meat in the morning and bread and meat in the evening, and he would drink from the brook. It happened after a while that the brook dried up, because there was no rain in the land." (1 Kings 17:6-7, NASB)*

> *"The LORD Himself goes before you; He will be*
> *with you. He will never leave you nor forsake you.*
> *Do not be afraid or discouraged." (Deuteronomy*
> *31:8, BSB)*

The Batting Cage Dream

My son-in-law and daughter were visiting our home when
he had a dream he didn't understand. "It is about you,
Bruce," he said.

We were at a baseball park and I was in a batter's box that
had a batting cage with a mechanized pitcher. Whatever
was thrown at me I would hit – every ball. They couldn't get
me out of the cage; I just kept batting the balls. He didn't
know what the dream meant.

A baseball has 216 stitches. While there are other meanings
for the number 216, the way I interpreted this dream was
that whatever the world throws at me, I hit it on the head
with a double (2) portion of God's love (16).

To explain further, in the Bible, numbers are used to convey
spiritual meaning in a language all their own, and the let-
ters are also words and concepts that can be used either lit-
erally or symbolically. Sixteen is the number of love. [6] It
was because of the love of God that Jesus was nailed to the
cross for the sin of the world. The cross manifested the love
of God for all mankind, *"For God so loved the world that He gave*

His only begotten Son, that whoever believes in Him shall not perish but have everlasting life" (John 3:16, NKJV). There are sixteen characteristics of love in 1 Corinthians 13:4-8, the great "Love Chapter." The book of John in the New Testament uses the Greek word *agape (divine love)* precisely sixteen times.

White Horse Company

In 2017, I went to a Conference in Branson, Missouri. When we arrived in town, my friend David and I went to the Flat Iron restaurant. The hostess said it would be ten minutes before we could get a table. We sat at a bench to wait. We were visiting and David went to get a menu. He came back and said the hostess told him it would be longer because several buses with a total of 144 people had just arrived.

I exclaimed, "144!"

> *"Then I looked, and behold, the Lamb was standing on Mount Zion, and with Him one hundred and forty-four thousand, having His name and the name of His Father written on their foreheads." (Revelation 14:1, NASB)*

The waitress finally seated us. As I passed by the hostess, I heard her say, "Of course, of course." I turned and looked at her. What I thought of instantly was Mr. Ed, the talking, white horse. I told David and he looked up the theme song of the Mr. Ed show.

Revelation 19:11-16 speaks of the White Horse Company of believers – the armies of heaven arrayed in fine linen, following Christ on white horses. The conference we were attending was such a company of overcoming believers. Prophecies often happen through people who don't even realize what they are saying. The Father talks to His children through other people's words and actions. He gives His children eyes to see, ears to hear, and hearts to perceive His word of truth as it is revealed — the Word of Life.

> *"And the armies which were in heaven followed him upon white horses, clothed in fine linen, white and clean." (Revelation 19:14, KJV)*

> *"The LORD said to me, "Son of man, mark well, see with your eyes and hear with your ears all that I say to you concerning all the statutes of the house of the LORD and concerning all its laws; and mark well the entrance of the house, with all exits of the sanctuary." (Ezekiel 44:5, NASB)*

> *"To him who overcomes I will grant to sit with Me on My throne, as I also overcame and sat down with My Father on His throne." (Revelation 3:21, NKJV)*

As we finished eating, I walked up the hostess and said, "Of course, of course," and told her I saw Jesus Christ.

I also told her, "He just spoke to me through you. You were prophesying. Even if I tried to explain it, you wouldn't understand."

She replied, "He did!" She was smiling and was all bright-eyed. God was showing me His sovereignty. When we were back at our hotel, I was pondering what had just happened at the restaurant. We were staying at the Seven Gables Inn – a building with all white brick. Horses stay in stables – rhymes with gable. God cares about details. As we are awake, aware, and alert in discernment and listen to His Spirit, He reveals more of the truth to us.

Telling My Story of Jesus

"We ought always to give thanks to God for you, brethren, as is only fitting, because your faith is greatly enlarged, and the love of each one of you toward one another grows ever greater;" (2 Thessalonians 1:3, NASB)

Tell Everyone Without Partiality

Jim and I were working at a place in Darfur, Minnesota where a heavily tattooed young man was upset with us. When we were on the job at his place, we left some nails in a board that were in a pile of wood we scrambled to pick up and set aside due to a rainstorm. We intended to finish the job at a later time. I decided I wouldn't tell him I had seen Jesus, since he was so upset.

One night soon after this happened, I had a dream. Diane and I found a lost twelve-year-old boy in an outside building. I told her, "Let's put some straw down. He'll be comfortable here." The next night I was dreaming again. I told Diane, "We shouldn't leave that boy down here in the shed. We should bring him up to the house." I woke up and thought about the dream. The twelve-year-old boy represents the tattooed, young man Jim and I were working for. He was a man young in his faith. Even if I thought he was a "lost" child, I should "bring him to the house." I should tell him about Christ. I am not supposed to judge people on where they are at in their faith. I was instructed to tell everyone; it was a lesson I needed to learn.

When I went back to work at the young man's place, I told him about seeing Jesus. His answer was, "My mother would think you are crazy." Then he talked about how he was raised in the Baptist church and gave me a history of his life. He didn't disbelieve me. I gave him some spiritual materials to read. He had a change of heart. From then on, he called me "brother." His change of heart was the work of the Holy Spirit.

Talking to Vendors

On the job, I talk to vendors, etc. about my experiences with Jesus. One man told me that he was impressed with how I handled tough situations on the job, going out of my way to help and was kind. He had told people I was one of the best contractors he'd worked with.

I buy carpentry materials from a local business in St. James, Minnesota. A rep from there goes along when I bid on jobs. If I tell people I saw Jesus Christ, he backs me up by saying, "I've known Bruce for thirty years and he isn't nuts. He wouldn't make anything up." I really appreciate his loyalty.

Perspective Change

In the Rochester, Minnesota Lowe's store, I told my story of seeing Jesus to a cashier. She said she had been a Christian and was now a Buddhist.

"Are you kidding me?" she said, when I told her I saw Jesus Christ. "I've got to go home and tell my parents this story." It changed her perspective.

I believe God leads me to talk to certain people to make a difference in their lives, just like He made a difference in mine when I was praying to be released from fear.

Afraid to Tell

There are people I share with that also share their own stories, but they often say, "Don't tell anyone." They are afraid to share their stories. I was told to "go and tell" so I am being obedient.

When I first saw Jesus, at a lady's place south of Butterfield, I didn't tell her anything about the encounter. I only told

Jim what was going on. Later, I went to tell that lady what had happened. She was kind of scared; I told her not to be scared. Then she felt comfortable enough to share her story of how she felt the presence of her husband, who had passed away some years ago.

Too Shocked to Stand

I went to see some people who had hired me to do carpentry for them. We became friends, and I told them about seeing Jesus. When I was finished, the man and I stood up, but his wife was so in awe of the story that she couldn't even stand up right away – she seemed like she was in paralyzed shock. She knew I wouldn't tell a story like that if it wasn't true. She needed to process the information. I hugged them and told them Christ loves them.

Were You There?

I sat with my cousins at a picnic table and told them I saw Jesus Christ. One of the cousins said, "That's quite a story." He went to see his brother-in-law and was making fun of me, "Did you hear about Bruce seeing Jesus Christ? I think he's flipped out of his mind."

The response was, "Were you there? How can you make fun of him if you weren't there? Why would he say something like that if it wasn't true?" It feels good when people defend my integrity and confirm to those who are skeptical that I wouldn't make up a story.

Root Canal

I was at the dentist to have a root canal. I talked to the dentist and receptionist about seeing Jesus Christ and hearing God's voice. He said to me, "Where does it say in the Scriptures that you need to hear the voice of the Lord?" I went home and looked up the Scriptures, and wrote them down so the next time I went back, I was able to give them to him. I teased the dentist and said, "God ordained that I would come back a second time so I could give these Scriptures to you." I wasn't excited about having a root canal, but was glad I could give him the Scripture verses to ponder.

Hearing God's voice is about focus and awareness: focusing attention on Him and being aware of His presence; desiring Him to speak to you. Sometimes His still, small voice is not easy to separate from one's own mind. It is good to keep records and ask for confirmation. When our minds are renewed, then our consciences will always be in full agreement with the voice of God. If we have any idols in our hearts, then we won't want to hear or agree with God's voice. An idol of the heart is any hidden motive or desire that prevents us from seeing truth or from seeing God as He really is. Heart idolatry prevents a person from understanding the merciful nature of God.

> *"In your distress, when all these things happen to you in days to come and you return to the LORD your God, **then you will hear his voice.**" (Deuteronomy 4:30, ISV)*

> *"Come, let us bow down in worship, let us kneel before the LORD our Maker; for he is our God and we are the people of his pasture, the flock under his care. Today, **if only you would hear his voice,**" (Psalm 95:6-7, NIV)*

> *"Son of man, these men have set up their **idols in their hearts** and have put right before their faces the stumbling block of their iniquity. Should I be consulted by them at all?" (Ezekiel 14:3, NASB)*

Sharing in a Sunday School Class

I went to speak in a Sunday School class. The teacher said, "Share your faith." I shared my story about seeing Jesus. The children and the other adults in the room just looked at me and really paid attention. I shared that the stories in the Bible actually happened to people. They are true, not just stories. They are stories about faith in God. I told them to share their faith in school and wherever they go. If someone is hurting, step up to them and help them; be a friend to them.

Lemonade Stand

When I talk to children, I like to get down on my knees at their level. At a lemonade stand near my home, I told the children selling the lemonade that I saw Jesus and that He loves them. I take the opportunity when I am prompted by the Spirit to share my story with all ages, young and old alike.

Sharing with Pastors

"Now when they saw the boldness of Peter and John, and perceived that they were uneducated, common men, they were astonished. And they recognized that they had been with Jesus." (Acts 4:13, ESV)

Hearing His Voice Through Music

Often on Sunday mornings, I will go to different churches in small towns. I remember hearing in the Spirit the song, "Will You Go with Me?" by Josh Turner. That was an encouragement to me from the Father. Whenever I hear music, song lyrics, and song titles in my spirit, I go and search it out to see what the Father is saying to me. It is one way He gets my attention and speaks to me.

God often speaks to us through things and people around us. He speaks through songs and headlines, movies, and the books we read.

Foot-Washing

I taught Sunday School for a few years and was Sunday School superintendent for two years. I also served on the church council for many years and was chair of the board during my last five years of service. In these roles, I worked closely with pastors. I knew the Father wanted me to share my story with pastors as He directed me.

Not long after I washed my pastor's feet *(on day four),* I was at a church meeting. The group representing ten to twelve churches was there to discuss finances and consider consolidating churches. I could see Jesus sitting at the next table. Jesus and I began chit-chatting in the spirit. One of the pastors began to speak. Then I heard from Jesus, "She needs a foot-washing."

Not long after that meeting, my parents and I went to a Lutheran church in Comfrey, Minnesota. The pastor was sitting in a pew, waiting for the service to begin. I went to her and asked if I could meet with her sometime. She said, "OK." I set up an appointment and met with her at the parsonage in St. James. I came with my foot-washing supplies; she wasn't aware of this. She invited me in. I told her I was supposed to wash her feet. She said, "They're kind of dirty."

"That doesn't matter," I replied. "I'm supposed to wash your feet."

I started washing her feet and said, "I'm a servant of the Lord."

"You **are** a servant of the Lord because you are washing my feet," she replied.

I was kneeling so when I finished, I asked permission to stand up. I began telling her the story of seeing Jesus Christ and being filled with the fire of God. She chuckled as if it was a big joke. When I finished the story, I packed my foot-washing supply bags and went home.

I called her later on, wanting to meet with the St. James Ministerial Association. She said, "Well, I'll see about it."

Later on, she said, "They'll let you speak."

Sharing at the Ministerial Association Meeting

I was nervous. Jim said, at the last minute, that he would go with me. Jesus often sent his disciples two by two.

> *Mark 6:7, NLT: "And he called his twelve disciples together and began sending them out two by two, giving them authority to cast out evil spirits."*

Jim and I met and went to the meeting. I prayed and asked for the Father's guidance that He would speak through us. We went in and met the chairperson. She said she'd give us fifteen minutes. We went into the fireside room where they were meeting.

When it was my turn on the agenda, I stood and gave each one a Lutheran hymnal, stating that I was raised in the West Sveadahl Lutheran Church. I told them Jesus appeared to me. Two female pastors started laughing. I told them my story and told them I was instructed to come. The Presbyterian pastor said to me, "You have a lot of stamina and strength to stand before us."

"I came in faith because He told me to come," I replied. After I said that, it became really quiet in the room. I asked them to stand. I went to each one and gave them a hug and kiss on the cheek and said, "Jesus loves you."

The pastor said, "You forgot Jim." So, I went to Jim and took his face in my hands and kissed him on both cheeks. After that, we packed up and went to work.

I'm Just a Man

I went to visit a former pastor of the church I belonged to and brought some spiritual literature along. We knew each other quite well. When I knocked on the door, the husband and wife greeted me and invited me into the kitchen to visit. I told them my story. They listened attentively and were very interested. The wife stared at me. I told them, "I'm just a man." I gave them literature and we said our goodbyes with hugs.

Visiting at a Church Auction

Later on, this same former pastor came to the church building auction. We talked, and he was very upset and discouraged. He told me, "I'm filled with the Holy Spirit too." *(The literature states that we have the earnest of the Spirit and will be filled with the fullness of the Spirit when we are mature overcomers.)*

> *"In whom ye also trusted, after that ye heard the word of truth, the gospel of your salvation: in whom also after that ye believed, ye were sealed with that holy Spirit of promise, Which is the earnest of our inheritance until the redemption of the purchased possession, unto the praise of his glory." (Ephesians 1:13-14, KJV)*

> *"Now he which stablisheth us with you in Christ, and hath anointed us, is God; Who hath also sealed us, and given the earnest of the Spirit in our hearts." (2 Corinthians 1:22, KJV)*

> *"And He gave some as apostles, and some as prophets, and some as evangelists, and some as pastors and teachers, for the equipping of the saints for the work of service, to the building up*

> *of the body of Christ; until we all attain to the*
> *unity of the faith, and of the knowledge of the*
> *Son of God, <u>to a mature man, to the measure of</u>*
> *<u>the stature which belongs to the fullness of Christ</u>."*
> *(Ephesians 4:11-13, NASB)*

Then he said, "I believe you, Bruce, that you did have this experience." He knew me as an honest person.

You Expect Us to Believe This?

I went to a church in St. James and told the pastor about the things I had seen and heard. In response, he challenged me and was not really accepting the message I shared. I gave him some literature and stepped back, not wanting to push anything. Some friends in that church, that I had known for years, were also skeptical and said, "You expect us to believe this?" These were people I'd known since I was a child. They were kind to me, but not totally buying my story.

Sometime later, I was in St. James buying gas and the skeptical St. James pastor drove up. I didn't recognize who he was at first. When he walked near me, he said, "Hello Bruce." Then I remembered his face. He came over and asked me about the three feasts.

I shared a summary of the three feasts with him: The <u>Passover</u> was when the Israelites left Egypt (Exod. 12). <u>Pentecost</u> is in Acts 1-2. Now we are looking forward to

Tabernacles (Feast of Booths – Leviticus 23). Individually (personally), Passover (justification) is when you become born again (John 3) and are justified by genuine faith in the blood of the Lamb – you believe Christ saved you. He was the Passover Lamb, killed at Passover in 33 A.D. "once for all" (Heb. 7:27). Pentecost (sanctification) is the baptism of the Holy Spirit — when you are hearing the voice of the Lord and are in training – learning to be led by the Holy Spirit. At Pentecost, the Lord chose to establish His name in the new temple of our bodies – writing His law in our hearts. *"Do you not know that you are the temple of God and that the Spirit of God dwells in you?" (1 Corinthians 3:16, NKJV).* The third feast, Tabernacles (glorification), will be fulfilled at the second coming of Christ, when we reach full maturity, have the mind of Christ, and receive our glorified, immortal bodies (2 Cor. 5:1-4). Until then, we are in a time of preparation, looking forward to what is ahead with the faith of overcomers waiting to inherit all that God has for us (1 Cor. 15: 12-28, 50-58). We overcome when we come into agreement with Him and obey His voice. We are learning to walk in lovingkindness. We are taking on His character and are becoming LIKE HIM. That is what Sonship is all about – to do only as He would do, to listen to His voice, and speak as He tells us. It is all about HIM and His will, not about us.

Then the pastor said, "Tell me about your experience of seeing Jesus Christ." I told him about being baptized with the fire of the Spirit, as John the Baptist proclaimed. I told the pastor I had holy communion with Christ. Then He told me to go tell His people. After that, I said to the pastor, "If Jesus told you to go tell people, would you do it? I'll tell you what I thought when He told me to go tell people. I thought, they'll think I'm crazier than a fruitcake and have flipped out. I've been faithful because He told me to."

"It's better to be faithful than not do what He asks. I've never had an experience like that," he replied. Then he left.

Vision of Snow

One morning, I was lying in bed meditating and I saw a vision of myself standing in the kitchen looking out the east window. I noticed the snow was coming down at an angle from the south. I thought the Father was telling me it was snowing outside; however, when I went into the kitchen and looked out the window, there was no snow. The sky was clear. I wondered what the Father was telling me.

Dark clouds get transformed into snow, symbolizing purity and cleanness. It is an example of transformation so we might reflect God in our lives. Scripture references to snow are found in some of the most beautiful passages of the Bible.

> *"Purify me with Hyssop, and I shall be clean;*
> *Wash me, and I shall be whiter than snow."*
> *(Psalm 51:7, NASB)*

"Come now, let us reason together, says the LORD:
though your sins are like scarlet, they shall be as
white as snow; though they are red like crimson,
they shall become like wool." (Isaiah 1:18, ESV)

He put in my heart the message that the truth of the gospel is coming.

A week or two later, I went to another church to talk to the pastor before the Sunday service. When the service ended, he invited me to come to the Bible class where they were studying Psalm 22. At the end of the class, he asked me to share my story. Those in attendance listened attentively and were receptive. I realized the vision of the snow was the Father showing me that I would have this window of opportunity to share my story.

Asked to Leave

One Sunday morning, I felt led by the Holy Spirit to visit a church in another town about an hour and a half from where I live. The message that morning was about false teachers and the importance of being discerning when people sometimes insert man-made teachings alongside the Scriptures to fit their particular beliefs. It was a good sermon that I agreed with.

After the service, I saw a friend talking to the pastor in the lobby of the church. She didn't know I was going to be there.

When she saw me, she was very surprised and motioned me to come over and introduced me to the pastor. I told him that I saw Jesus Christ. He said he wanted to hear the story so I shared further. My friend was listening to our conversation. When I used the term "Age of Tabernacles," he got very red in the face and upset. He immediately said that was false teaching because that term wasn't in the Bible and asked me to leave. I hugged him and left and went to my car, hoping my friend would still be my friend. I learned later that the pastor told her to stay away from me because I was spreading false teaching.

Thankfully, when we spoke later, she said that she knows I am not spreading false teaching and that the "Age of Tabernacles" is a legitimate term to use just like the term "Trinity," which isn't directly mentioned in the Bible. Sometimes, when a term isn't familiar or isn't being frequently used, people don't understand it so they become afraid and extremely cautious. It is important to be like the Bereans and search the Scriptures to see if what is being taught is accurate before judging too harshly.

Later that day, I was thinking of Elvis Presley and his music on YouTube. Because his style of music was new, it wasn't accepted by many, especially the church. When I went to bed, I was meditating on the rejection he experienced when he introduced a new kind of music. Just like that, I heard in my spirit, "The Father is very proud of you."

A few days later in the spirit, I saw a pure, white light and I followed the pure, white light within me ... then, I saw a swan. I knew this was a sign from the Father. I wasn't sure what it meant at the time. Since then, I learned that the spiritual meaning of a swan is about maintaining grace in communication with other people. The swan is a symbol of purity, beauty, grace, love, elegance, and balance. I have nothing against any pastor who is not ready to receive my testimony.

Timing is Important

I went to my aunt's funeral and talked to the pastor of her church. He was very open and receptive to my story of seeing Jesus Christ. He was interested in how Jesus talked to me, using wording that's in the hymnal. He communicates with me in terms I can understand and am familiar with. The pastor asked if I had told my story to my cousins (my aunt's children). I said, "No, I have not done that." It did not work out that day because they were focused on the funeral and it was not the right time or location.

You Should Be Proud of Your Son

I saw the pastor of the Comfrey Lutheran Church when I went to the bank one day. We had met previously at church meetings. I said to him, "I have an interesting story to tell you." Then I briefly told him of seeing Jesus Christ. He listened and didn't have a problem with it. We hugged and left the bank.

Later, I visited his church. He came to greet me because he had met me previously. I would quote Scriptures to him related to Tabernacles. He would go home and check it out (like the Bereans) and research what I had said.

> *"These (Bereans) were more noble than those in Thessalonica, in that they received the word with all readiness of mind, and searched the scriptures daily, whether those things were so." (Acts 17:11, KJV)*

My parents went to his church in Comfrey for a funeral. After the funeral, they had lunch and sat with the pastor's sister and brother-in-law to visit. The pastor found out they were my parents; he told them, "You should be very proud of your son. What Bruce has told me and the Scriptures he quotes, I can find it in the Bible."

The pastor told me that anytime I wanted to come over to discuss Scripture, I was welcomed. One evening I went to a visitation in Comfrey. Afterwards, I went to the pastor's home. His wife answered the door and invited me in. The pastor and I went into the living room and visited. We discussed my experiences – what I've seen and heard. He asked me, "How do you hear the Spirit's voice? Audible or inside?"

I said, "It's inside."

He said that he's had an experience of God speaking to him. Then he said, "Bruce, do you realize you're a messenger of God?"

"Yes, I do," I replied. "I was told by God to share experiences with you and others."

Answering Questions

———

"Moreover, besides being wise himself, the Teacher
taught people what he had learned by listening,
making inquiries, and composing many prov-
erbs." (Ecclesiastes 12:9, ISV)

After Bruce shared his story, I (Annette) asked him
the following questions:

**AR: What is the most important message Jesus wants
you to share?**

BH: That He is real and He loves everyone. He wants a
relationship with us.

He wants us to walk in His likeness. We are to be an expres-
sion of Him on this earth. When someone sees you – they
should see Jesus. Jesus wants us to hear His voice and obey,
to trust Him.

AR: How has seeing Jesus changed your life?

BH: Jesus Christ is on my mind continually. He is very real to me all the time. The message He asked me to share is my most important topic of conversation wherever I go. At first it was difficult to even think of sharing because of wondering how my story would be received. Now, years later, and after sharing many hundreds of times with many different people all across the United States, I look forward to telling people how much Jesus loves them and how real He is. He wants to be the best friend we could ever have. He suffered and died for us to save us from our sins. His love is unconditional.

AR: Did you speak to Jesus with actual verbal words, or just in your spirit?

BH: We simultaneously communicated our thoughts and emotions and understood each other perfectly, even though we did not use verbal language. God doesn't need verbal language to communicate.

AR: Since no one else saw Jesus but you, describe what it was like to see Him "in the spirit."

BH: When you dream at night, it can be very real. What is happening is just as real as if you were awake. When I saw Jesus, it was like a daytime dream or vision. I was wide awake and going about my day, but was experiencing a real encounter with Jesus. He removed the veil and opened my eyes to see Him, though He remained invisible to everyone else.

> *"But we all, with unveiled face, beholding as in a mirror the glory of the Lord, are being transformed into the same image from glory to glory, just as by the Spirit of the Lord." (2 Corinthians 3:18)*

AR: You mentioned Jesus made you laugh. Please explain further.

BH: He just made me laugh and feel comfortable. He tried to make me open up, let down my guard, and relax. He put great joy in my heart and a smile on my face. It was like being with the best friend in the world and having fun with him/her, being vulnerable with him/her without judgement or criticism.

On the Friday morning of my eight-day experience, I was sitting on the edge of my bed getting dressed for the day. Jesus was sitting next to me and said, "What are you going to do today?" It was raining so I said I was going to work in the shop. No matter where I went or what I did, He was there with me. I remember constantly thinking, *What's so special about me that I am chosen to have this experience?* I felt like I could tell Him everything. He had such great love; there was nothing to fear. In my time with Him, I realized the importance of uplifting someone rather than tearing him/her down.

AR: Have you faced many challenges because of your experience?

It was tough to step forward and tell others what happened. I wondered, *What are people going to think about this?* It took a lot of courage. I was a shy person – definitely not bold. Then I became bold and straightforward – not backing down. I had no idea if my parents would support me or reject me.

There have been challenges since this happened because there are people close to me who are not supportive and don't want to accept my story. I know I need to continue to share because I was told by God to share. *"We ought to obey God rather than men." (Acts 5:29, KJV)*

Just because some people don't have ears to hear doesn't make me stop sharing. If I tell someone I saw Jesus Christ and there's no response, I don't force the story on them.

I often wonder how anyone can say my story is not true if they weren't there. Jim was there with me. I gave him a play by play of what was happening. You can't know that much detail if you aren't seeing it. He believed me because he knows me and knows I wouldn't make anything up.

Family Testimonies

"For He established a testimony in Jacob and appointed a law in Israel, which He commanded our fathers to teach to their children, that the coming generation would know them—even children yet to be born—to arise and tell their own children that they should put their confidence in God, not forgetting His works, but keeping His commandments." (Psalm 78:5-7, BSB)

AR: How has your encounter with Jesus affected your daughters and their families? How have their lives been impacted?

BH: It is important to me that they tell you in their own words how my encounter has impacted their lives. I would like you to interview them personally so that you can hear directly from them.

Bruce and I (Annette) traveled to Rochester, Minnesota to visit Jessica and Sandy and their husbands, so that I could meet them and hear them tell how Bruce's encounter with Jesus impacted their lives. Bruce chose not to be in the room when I interviewed each of them individually.

Here is how they responded to my questions:

JESSICA (daughter)

"At first, I wasn't bold in sharing the story with people.

"My dad saw Jesus just after I had my first child. It was years later, when I was pregnant with my third child, that I just had to have a garage sale before the birth. There was a lady that always came to my garage sales. This time she came and said, 'I just feel like I'm supposed to come back here for something.' Like a bolt of lightning, I knew that I was supposed to tell her about my dad seeing Jesus. It was my first time sharing the experience with someone outside of family and friends. She was thrilled (it was a revelation to her). She said she works with the elderly who would be so encouraged to hear this story. It was an eye-opening experience. Talking about our faith made us both feel like a million dollars.

"I sold an item on Facebook and the lady mentioned God, so I shared my dad's story with her. She said, 'I have something to share with you. I saw Jesus, too, when I was a little girl. I haven't even told my family. There are two spirits that follow me. I believe they are there to protect me.' I encouraged her to not be afraid to share her experience with her family. There's nothing to be scared of.

"I took a group of students to Camp Omega near Waterville, Minnesota. On the way there, we had so much time to talk. I brought cupcakes and said I was going to tell them stories. I shared the story about my dad seeing Jesus and told stories of God talking to me. Then I asked if someone had something to share. A boy in the back told about how his mom said she heard God's voice. She works at the Mayo Clinic in Rochester, Minnesota and was having a hard time with a patient. She heard God say to her that everything would be OK. I spoke with that mom later. I told her to believe that God does speak to us when we listen.

"I was in the Mayo courtyard with my daughter. A lady was sitting on a bench and was crying. We went over to talk to her. I hugged her and said, 'Everything is going to be OK. God loves you.' I kissed the top of her head, gave her another big hug, and said, 'Jesus is here with you.' She said, 'Thank you!' In the evening, I prayed for her again and said, 'God, please help that lady and tell her it's going to be OK.' God said ... 'You already did that for me.' I was excited to tell my husband, 'God talked to me.'

"I wanted to start a faith-based, short-term rental business. My husband was supportive of the idea. When I was thinking about the business one day, Jason Gray's song, 'Sparrows' was being played on the radio. The lyrics encouraged me, 'If God can take care of sparrows, He'll take care of you.' [7]

"We began looking for our first house in 2017. A cute, storybook house went on the market that we liked, but we met a roadblock because we found it right before the bidding period ended. We submitted a bid anyway and said we'd pay a little above asking price. There were six offers. The realtor said there was no chance because it was just too late.

"Then I listened to a pastor say, 'Pray specifically for what you want.' I did that, 'Father, if it is Your will for me to start this business, please open this door.' God answered my prayer. I got the call – 'The house is yours if you want it.'

"It was God's plan that we have this family business, coveredbyfaithrentals.com. It's like reserving at a hotel, but it's a house. We can reserve one night or more. Our houses are: Storybook House, Family House, Trust House, and Blessed House. They are located within walking distance of the Mayo Clinic and St. Mary's Hospital in Rochester, Minnesota.

"Often entire families need a place to stay. A hotel room is too small. We have big houses that will accommodate a family, giving children a place to play, watch videos, play games, and relax. They can cook and wash clothes. Just like being at home.

"We have learned so many important lessons. The children are learning about work, values, and discipline. They earn money. It's been a great way to teach my children. The feedback from the people who we bought the Storybook home from was very encouraging. They said, 'We are so happy with what you have done to this place.' We helped them; they helped us. God has led us more than we can ever imagine.

"When we have renters (often people who are patients at Mayo) and something needs to be fixed, we then have an opportunity to tell them about my dad seeing Jesus. It gives them a ray of hope and encouragement.

"We have met people who have had their own encounters with God and are happy to share their experiences with someone who will understand, someone who will be excited with them.

"We sometimes have renters who were not raised in the faith. When they are treated well, they want to learn more because they feel so loved and cared for. People say, 'You are a life saver.' I know that this is all God making the connections, putting people in our path, putting us in a place to be a blessing to others.

"My goal now is to tell people about Jesus. When I start talking with others, they also share stories. It is a fun connection. God gives us the words of wisdom when we need them.

"My children are seeing answers to prayer. We talk about this during devotions where I read a children's Bible to them after supper. Their faith is strengthened when God answers their prayers.

"Our daughter had nightmares and she prayed to God. She hasn't had nightmares since.

"Our family was walking in Cub Foods after church one Sunday with my dad and he said, 'Jesus is walking with us.' We just kept shopping. It felt awesome and was such a unique experience to think of having Jesus walk with us in the grocery store.

"When I think back to when I was a little girl, I remember being really scared of death. I was home alone in a fetal position, crying. I was scared that I was going to die. I felt the Holy Spirit come over me and I settled right down.

"Shortly after I was married, I was afraid to have children and the Holy Spirit came over me and helped me to be OK with it. I now have four beautiful, healthy children.

"Since my dad's encounter, I'm definitely more confident, bold, and comfortable talking to others about him seeing

Jesus. This is real; it has happened in real life. This is more than what you hear on Sunday morning. As a child, I remember asking, 'Why do we only see Jesus in Bible stories and not now in our world?' Little did I know there was a plan to answer that question later in life. It is all about His timing."

DARIN (Jessica's husband)

"Bruce's encounter has definitely impacted us a lot. To hear of someone going through an experience like that – someone so close – it warms your heart to know there is that proof out there, that there is a God. We knew it, but to know it so personally, is impactful.

"Throughout the years, as Bruce has been changed and impacted, seeing his continued growth for knowledge, I have grown and piggybacked on it. I do more reading and studying, trying to absorb knowledge. It's been a fun journey. Bruce and I read some of the same things so we have good conversations.

"It is interesting going with Bruce to places to see how his visiting with people plays out as he talks to complete strangers. Some laugh at his face and walk away. Some act like best friends, hugging at the end because it's been a fun conversation. There's been the broad spectrum.

"It is enjoyable to listen to him telling people his story and seeing their immediate reactions. I chime in when I can with the conversation.

"As Jessica's husband, I see more boldness in her. We try to follow suit like Bruce and not be afraid to share. We tell co-workers and friends at church that my father-in-law has seen Jesus.

"Jessica has definitely become more confidently bold over the years in her approach. She's not afraid to share stories. It comes to play a lot in our rental business. We call it God-sightings.

"Many of our faith-based rental business guests are in crisis situations and need someone to connect with. They need to be encouraged. We try to welcome all and be a comfort to them. If they are open to hear, we will share.

"We focus on having homes within walking distance of Mayo. We are thankful to rent our homes to patients, but we will definitely take anyone.

"We are keeping our eyes open to how God is moving in this world. It is easy to focus on the task at hand, on the day-to-day, but to realize that He is here and interacting with us is special. We continually keep our eyes and ears open to the reality of what He is doing in the moment. It would be nice to have an encounter like Bruce's, but for now, just seeing how God works in our day-to-day lives directly is a blessing.

"It's been fun and has definitely helped my faith grow."

SANDY (daughter)

"At first, my dad's encounter didn't impact me as much. As life has progressed, I am less afraid and have found opportunities to more freely talk about God. He is the reason I have what I have. He is the reason I am where I am today. It has opened my eyes to have a personal connection with God and people. I know others can have that personal connection too. All may not be perfect in life, but if you reflect back, you understand why you went through that hard time. You learn from it and you can teach others. God has put that on my heart to do – to help others.

"When I am with my dad and he talks to people about His encounter, I am his second witness. When he and I went to Hawaii, he was spreading God's Word to others. I was able to say, 'I'm his daughter. My dad isn't crazy. I know he had this experience.' It made those listening more comfortable and gave my dad credibility. He appreciated the backup.

"My dad is very bold when he talks to people about God. I freely share my faith, but I don't push it on others. My approach is that I look for an opportunity as the conversation progresses to share with them about my dad's encounter.

It is easier for me to do it that way. When I share my faith, it helps people become comfortable talking about their own experiences with God.

"Bad things could have happened to me when I lived in California, but they didn't because I was protected by God. I see now how God was taking care of me. God is in our lives and He is there for us all the time. Things will fall into place in His time and in His way.

"Years ago, when I was in training at Mayo, we were almost at the end of our training. There was a lady in the training class who sat next to other people but didn't tell any of them that she couldn't do the job that we were training for. The day she sat next to me, she broke down and cried. She said, 'I can't believe I'm telling you this.' I asked her if her other job was still available, and it was. I told her that it was OK for her to tell the trainer that she didn't get it. If this was not for her, it would be better to go back to her other job. I told her to tell the trainer that she would be leaving. I said, 'There is no point in continuing to do this if this is not the right path for you.' I was thankful she opened up to me. She could have opened up to anyone else in the training, but she opened up to me. She realized I was honest and had a pure heart. She didn't sense a barrier between us. This wasn't the first time this type of experience happened to me.

"Before I met my husband, John, I had some pretty chal-lenging relationships and bad things took place. As a result,

I was able to help others get through their horrible relationships and helped them realize they could do better.

"During one of those bad relationships with someone who was very rude, I wanted to sell wine. He told me not to, but I went against him and decided to do it anyway. There was a reason I felt that I needed to have this job, because that was the path where I would meet my husband. We started hanging out and we were just friends for two years before we dated. John is very strong in his faith and has a solid connection with God. John heard about my dad's encounter with Jesus and said he needed to meet him because of a vision. He met him in the park and visited with him during the time when we were just friends.

"John had been in bad relationships too, but those relationships have made both of us realize what we needed in life, and we were able to more easily recognize a good person. I now know that I met my soulmate because I went through those bad relationships. It's important to find the good in the bad. Many people don't realize that there are reasons we go through certain things. Having really strong faith allows you to do that.

"Almost two years ago, I was going to lose my job at Mayo. I was scared, even though I knew that whatever happened God would be there for me. Whatever I would go through was for a reason. I ended up having more than one interview. I felt strongly, in the process of interviewing, that I was supposed to have a supervisor who I could talk to about God. At first, I didn't realize it; however, in my job at the time, I sat next to a lady who helped me become strong in God and faith and what that all really meant. As I had my fourth interview, I said to this lady, 'I know that God will take care of me, but how do I get rid of this fear that I'm going to be left without a job?' She said that I wasn't really giving it to God. I said, 'You are absolutely right; I'm not giving it to Him. I'm not trusting Him a hundred percent.' That night, I was reading some very encouraging words on LinkedIn and Facebook. I read that you don't see the sparrows worrying about where they are going to get their next meal. If God takes care of the birds, He surely is going to take care of you. From then on, things just started falling into place.

"Right after that, my husband said, 'There is a job that you are supposed to apply for that was just listed.' I went and looked but thought it was a different job. He didn't lose that feeling so the next day he said again that the job was still open. I found the job he was referring to and applied for it. I didn't have to contact the hiring manager to have a formal interview. I was contacted just from my application, and everything fell into place.

"It is important to believe in signs and God working through people. It was interesting because, just before I was hired for this job, I met the lady that helped me realize I should have a connection with God through the supervisor. It's powerful when you see how God and your life can be aligned. It is important to believe that God really provides opportunities for you. You have to keep your eyes wide open to see it. I just needed to trust Him. The way to do that is to honestly believe that He provides for you. I don't know if I would have the vision of how God works in each situation if my dad hadn't had his encounter fifteen years ago. It has opened my eyes to see how God is real in our lives.

"My children, ages six and four, know who God is and that He provides for us. They know we have what we have because of Him. When we go through green lights, we always thank God. They say, 'Thank you, God.' They know He is there, that He will protect them and we need to pray to Him. That is what we have instilled in our children.

"Having strong faith in God during this COVID-19 pandemic is important. In times of need, when people have to come together and help one another, we see good deeds being done. More people realize what we are here on this earth for – to be a blessing to each other. I know I am here to help other people and spread God's Word.

"It is because of our connection to God that people seek us out. It's about who He has made us to be. They realize that we are safe, and that we truly care and want to help. When we find the right opportunity to talk about God, it gives them permission to share their faith. He puts people in our paths just at the right time. God's timing of the events in our lives is perfect. We need to go through difficult things sometimes to bring us to a place where we see our need for Him. After I met my husband, my life has fallen into place. I was able to see his value because of what I had been through previously.

"My path is laid out for me and I know I will be taken care of. God is sovereign. Whatever barrier I go through, I will get through it in the end."

JOHN (Sandy's husband)

"Sandy and I were friends first before we got married. She told me about her dad's experience.

"I had a vision that I HAD to speak to Sandy's father at a certain park, at a certain table. I told her about the vision; we set it up and that's how I met Bruce. He told me about his encounter.

"Then Sandy and I dated, and got married.

"We both rely on God more. We just always know that He's always got our backs. There is a reason for everything. We pray more, about little things and the big things. Communication is important.

"I hear stories from Jessica and Sandy about how they enjoy helping people.

"When Bruce first told me the story, I automatically believed him. Why would somebody lie about something like an encounter with Jesus? What would you have to gain to make the story up?

"Ever since I heard his story, I look around for signs. Even people that don't believe have signs; they just don't know how to explain them.

"I've always had God in my life, but not to this extent. Bruce's encounter has affected me a lot. It has opened my eyes. It's not only the big things that God does; it's the little things too. I thank Him now more than I ever have.

"When God spoke to Bruce, He told him to spread the word. Obviously, he affected our family. He shared with us, then we share with others. It's a chain reaction.

"I don't read the Bible every night. I don't have to go to church; I love going to church. I go because I want to. It's a daily walk with God.

"Bruce's encounter brought God up front to me. I think about God more. He affects my life more."

Bruce's Reflection

"So, in the present case I advise you: Leave these men alone. Let them go! For if their purpose or endeavor is of human origin, it will fail. But if it is from God, you will not be able to stop them. You may even find yourselves fighting against God." (Acts 5:38-39, BSB)

I called for God in prayer and He came to me. Even when there are challenges along the way, I know it is important for me to be obedient and share. There are definitely more blessings than difficulties because of my experience.

God chooses who He wants to choose to spread His truth. I may not fit some people's idea of a messenger, but in Jesus's day, He chose common fishermen to be His disciples. He often calls those who have learned from life's experiences that they need Him. I am a simple carpenter, a messenger from God. It's not easy to be simple. He told me to tell you; this is my divine appointment.

Saul was killing Christians before Jesus spoke to him as he journeyed to Damascus (Acts 9). He was commissioned by Jesus, received the name Paul, and became the apostle who wrote many of the New Testament books. God doesn't call the qualified; He qualifies the called.

Think about it ... What if this happened to you?

I was seeking to be free from fear – now I am sharing fearlessly and spreading the Gospel of the Kingdom – the good news of repentance, redemption, and restoration offered by God to all who will receive Christ.

Jesus desires to be glorified on earth as He is in heaven. In the Lord's Prayer, we recite, "Your kingdom come. Your will be done on earth as it is in heaven ... And forgive us our debts, as we also have forgiven our debtors," (Matt. 6:10,12) followed by "For if you forgive men their trespasses, your heavenly Father will also forgive you. But if you do not forgive men their trespasses, neither will your Father forgive yours" (Matt. 6:14-15, BSB). If we want to be forgiven in heaven, we must forgive on earth.

As I have grown in my relationship with the Lord Jesus Christ, I have learned about intercession and engaging in spiritual warfare on behalf of the church and the nation.

> *"Pray at all times in the Spirit with every prayer and request, and stay alert with all perseverance and intercession for all the saints." (Ephesians 6:18, CSB)*

God removed the "veil" from my heart so I could see God without the veil. I was given a unique and special experience that changed my life. I feel honored and humbled.

> *"For I reckon that the sufferings of this present time are not worthy to be compared with the glory which shall be revealed in us. For the earnest expectation of the creation eagerly waits for the revealing of the sons of God." (Romans 8:18-19, NKJV)*

> *"For us, however, God has drawn aside the **veil** through the teaching of the Spirit; for the Spirit searches everything, including the depths of the divine nature." (1 Corinthians 2:10, NKJV)*

I trust you have been blessed and encouraged in reading about my encounter with Jesus. Pray and ask Him to reveal Himself to you – He will be listening. Read, study, and obey His word – it is powerful and life-giving.

Annette's Comments

———

Jesus said, "You are My friends if you do what I command you." (John 15:14, NASB)

When I began this project, I didn't know Bruce very well. I just felt compelled to write his story since he was so believable. His unusual encounter needed to be in writing.

Christ was at the center of our daily lives in the godly Lutheran home where I grew up. It was definitely not a Sunday religion, rather a day-to-day walk with God. My parents believed fervently in the power of prayer, had morning and evening personal Bible reading, as well as family devotions after meals morning and evening. Having gone to parochial school during grades 3-12, I memorized many Scriptures and hymns. I remember watching the Billy Graham crusades on TV at a young age and found myself in tears when "Just As I Am" was sung during the altar call.

During my teen years, I made some unwise decisions that came with unpleasant consequences. I thank God that He had His eye on me, and led me to repent and yield my life to Him as Lord when I was nineteen. I know what it's like to be truly baptized in the Holy Spirit. What a life-changing experience. The Bible became very real to me. The Scriptures I memorized had new meaning. I felt like a sponge, soaking up every word. It was life-giving.

My journey through life was not easy. There were many challenges along the way, including my nineteen-year-old pregnant daughter, Rachel, being killed suddenly in a car crash. During that experience, I learned in an even deeper way just how much God loves us and provides everything we need in crisis situations. He gives us strength when we are in agony and asking "Why?" He is faithful and loves us passionately.

When I heard Bruce's story, I didn't question the reality of Jesus appearing to him, because God uses many ways to speak to people, to answer their prayers, and to help them to trust Him more. God knows best what to do in our lives to reveal Himself to us. He knows us better than we know ourselves. We must be tuned to the "right frequency" to hear the messages being sent to us from God.

"The wind blows where it wishes and you hear the sound of it, but you do not know where it comes

> *from or where it is going; so is everyone who is*
> *born of the Spirit." (John 3:8, NASB)*

Since I have spent more time with Bruce, and have had the opportunity to meet and visit with his daughters and their husbands, it is clearly evident that Bruce is the real deal. He is respectful, kind, and has been fun to work with. He has too much integrity and awe of the heavenly Father to make up a story. The facts are important to him. He clearly remembers the details and vividly recalls his emotions even fifteen years later. His memory is sharp, and it is evident that He is excited when people believe him.

This was a unique encounter with Jesus. The direction Bruce was given, to share the message with others, was not easy, particularly in the beginning. As time has progressed, Bruce has not wavered but has become increasingly bold. The responses have been far more positive than negative. That has been delightful for me to witness – at a restaurant, a conference, or on an Uber/shuttle ride. People's faces "light up" as they listen and then they begin to share their own stories of hearing from God in various ways. They are thrilled to have the opportunity to tell their own stories to someone who will not criticize them. They feel validated and liberated.

It is my belief that God can alter space, time, and dimension as He wills. I don't need to understand how it works, but I must believe that God is all in all and can do whatever

He pleases, when He pleases. As humans, we may not have the capacity to understand everything about God and His capabilities, but we know that He is creative and His love is inexhaustible.

> *"For by Him all things were created that are in heaven and that are on earth, visible and invisible, whether thrones or dominions or principalities or powers. All things were created through Him and for Him. And He is before all things, and in Him all things consist." (Colossians 1:16-17, NKJV)*

> *"Now when all things are made subject to Him, then the Son Himself will also be subject to Him who put all things under Him, that God may be all in all." (1 Corinthians 15:28, NKJV)*

> *"And there are diversities of activities, but it is the same God who works all in all." (1 Corinthians. 12:6, NKJV)*

I hope in reading this that you have learned the importance of believing that: 1) spiritual life is more important than physical life; 2) God is REAL, and is present and at work in our lives and in our world; 3) we are each a beautiful part of an intricate tapestry of love that God created when He made us.

Writing about God's amazing grace and desire to be our Savior and friend is inspiring. He wants to have a comfortable, loving, intimate relationship with each of us. The way we get close to another person is the same way we can get closer to Jesus.

> *"You will seek me and find me when you search for me with all your heart," (Jeremiah 29:13, NKJV)*

> *"Ask and it will be given to you; seek and you will find; knock and the door will be opened to you." (Matthew 7:7, NIV)*

> *"If you confess with your mouth, 'Jesus is Lord,' and believe in your heart that God raised Him from the dead, you will be saved." (Romans 10:9, CSB)*

> *"But as many as received Him, to them He gave the right to become children of God, to those who believe in His name." (John 1:12, NKJV)*

It is possible that you have read this story and realize that you don't have a personal relationship with Jesus Christ. You know ABOUT Him but you don't KNOW Him. We can know ABOUT Him in our minds, but our hearts haven't been transformed.

God's grace is amazing. He has provided the opportunity for you to have a personal relationship with Him. You have read in this story how He loves you and wants to walk and talk with you, and be your Savior and your best friend. If you would like to be born again and have Jesus as your Lord, you can say this prayer:

> *Dear God, I change my mind about who I want to be in charge of my life. I confess with my mouth that You, Jesus, are Lord, the ruler over all. You are the Christ, the Son of God. I believe Your blood that was shed on the cross washes away all my sin. I invite You, Jesus, to have first place in my heart and my life. Please make me clean. Restore me to a right relationship as a child of my heavenly Father. Fill me with Your Holy Spirit. Thank you, Lord, for Your cleansing blood! I now stand clean and white in Your presence. I pray this in Jesus's powerful name. Amen.*

True faith is believing God's promise that He will change our hearts by the power of the Holy Spirit. He promises to do the work in us, rather than us doing the work. We can't change ourselves, no matter how much good we try to do. He works in us, speaks to us, and leads us through His Spirit. Salvation is based on His oath to transform us, not on our well-intentioned vows. It is His work within us that changes our hearts so that we will no longer want to sin.

> *"But this is the covenant that I will make with the house of Israel after those days, says the LORD: I will put My law in their minds, and write it on their hearts; and I will be their God, and they shall be My people." (Jeremiah 31:33; Hebrews 8:10, NKJV)*

To grow in faith and the knowledge of the Lord Jesus Christ, it is important to read and study the Bible, fellowship with other Christians, and talk to Him in prayer. Listen carefully to the Holy Spirit's voice when He speaks to you and obey what He tells you to do. Make Him a priority. He wants us to love and serve one another, and be a blessing wherever we go.

God bless you in your day-by-day journey.

Delighted to be His daughter,

Annette Rode

If you would like to contact me, I can be reached via my website at **positivelifeattitudes.com**.

("Triumph in Tragedy" the story about my daughter Rachel's accident is also on my website.)

References

1 "In the Garden," lyrics by C. Austin Miles, 1912, Public Domain. *This work is in the **public domain** in the **United States** because it was published before January 1, 1925.*

2 "Here I am Lord. Is it I, Lord?" lyrics by Daniel Schutte; *With One Voice, A Lutheran Resource for Worship; #752. Permission was granted from Augsburg Fortress Publishing, Minneapolis, MN.*

3 "Thank the Lord and sing His praise; tell everyone what He has done," lyrics by Gerhard M. Cartford, b.1923; Post Communion Canticle, *Lutheran Book of Worship*, page 72. *Permission was granted from Augsburg Fortress Publishing, Minneapolis, MN.*

4 "Word of life, Jesus Christ, all glory to you!" *With One Voice, A Lutheran Resource for Worship;* Gospel Acclamation. Authors/translators of liturgical texts are acknowledged: Susan Palo Cherwien (b.1953), Gail Ramshaw (b.1947), Martin A. Seltz (b.1951),

and Frank Stoldt (b.1958). *Permission was granted from Augsburg Fortress Publishing, Minneapolis, MN.*

5   "Lift High the Cross," lyrics by George w. Kitchin, 1827-1902, *Lutheran Book of Worship, #377. Permission was granted from Augsburg Fortress Publishing, Minneapolis, MN.*

6   http://numerology.center/biblical_num-bers_number_16.php Biblical Numerology / Numerology Center

Number 16 is doubled from number 8 which is a symbol of spiritual purity and kindness. Number 16 is strongly associated with love and its manifestations. God's love can be reached not through merely obeying the Commandments physically, but also deeply spiritually believing in God, showing true love and being open to others. The spiritual meaning of God's laws and Commandments should be saved and kept in heart of a believer. The nature of physical and spiritual intent is shown in 8+8 which is 16. It leads us to one, whole and perfect love of God. Paul in the book to Corinthians told that there are 16 things connected to love that God has and that should be achieved by people as well. Love is kind, patient, non-jealous, humble, durable, non-egotistic, is not easy to evoke and has no dark intentions, joyful, forgiving and positive about the future, and it will never disappear. Love never behaves in a bad way, it never envies or desires others, it is full of hope.

https://www.biblestudy.org/bibleref/meaning-of-numbers-in-bible/16.html

Biblical Mathematics, Keys to Scripture Numerics by Ed. F. Vallowe, The Olive Press, 1998

The Numerical Structure of the Holy Bible by Charles Stockford, Jr., Page Publishing, Inc., 2016

7   "Sparrows"–Jason Gray. *Christian & Gospel* · SINGLE– "Sparrows" 3:27 Minutes. Released March 25, 2016. "Sparrows" is on the fifth studio album by Jason Gray, *Where the Light Gets In*. *Centricity Music* released the album on June 17, 2016.

CPSIA information can be obtained
at www.ICGtesting.com
Printed in the USA
LVHW050931091120
671147LV00011B/592

9 781632 213006